Africa's
Priceless Heritage

Africa's
Priceless Heritage

CLIFFORD CHAUKURA

authorHOUSE®

AuthorHouse™ UK
1663 Liberty Drive
Bloomington, IN 47403 USA
www.authorhouse.co.uk
Phone: 0800.197.4150

Published by AuthorHouse 04/07/2015

ISBN: 978-1-5049-3965-2 (sc)
ISBN: 978-1-5049-3966-9 (e)

Print information available on the last page.

DEDICATION

This book is dedicated with utmost passion to Wadzanayi Chaukura, my wife of twenty three years now. She is truly a priceless gift from the almighty God, a partner who propels me to hit success levels beyond my human imagination. I also dedicate this book to my three children, Sharon, Mercy and Ngonidzashe. These have assisted me to understand the dynamism of parenting in a turbulent socio-economic environment.

Finally I want to dedicate this valuable present to my varied readers who have enjoyed my other works which are selling on the market.

CONTENTS

FOREWORD

There is a myth that has kept many Africans at bay in terms of unleashing their personal potential in all the spheres of life. This has also paralyzed many as it has kept the Black Community from fully appreciating its rich heritage over the years. This myth is attributed (by its perpetrators) to the curse pronounced on Canaan by his grandfather, Noah (Gen 9:25). Since the Bible is definitely the Word of God and the standard by which all nations determine the truth we will begin from there and refer to its messages in many instances. The Bible teaches that it is only the truth which has a unique capacity to set humanity free (John 8:32).

It is my hope that all those who take time to read this book will be greatly enriched by the evidence of wide research which reveals the African's place in the great plan of God.

This work must be viewed as one of many attempts to put the myth to rest so that we all view all races as God views them. Spiritual assessment carry great weight in any culture hence it is of vital importance that Africa assesses itself on the basis of the Holy Bible and not on hearsay.

Clifford Chaukura.

ACKNOWLEDGEMENTS

I wish to express my heartfelt gratitude to Dr. Jonathan Musvosvi a fellow servant in the gospel ministry for his assistance in editing this research work. May I also acknowledge the positive contributions and support offered by Dr. R. Muzira.

I am also indebted to Eria Mazhura, a family friend whose positive influence and involvement in my career life has propelled me to achieve much needed success in ministry.

Most of all, I thank God who taught me from His Holy Word that I am fearfully and wonderfully made in His image.

INTRODUCTION

Some philosophers and theologians have been teaching the world that the Black pigmentation on the African skin was as a result of Ham being cursed by his father, Noah and consequently turning black, implying that Ham was originally white-skinned. Understandably, the Bible speaks about God's curse on Miriam, Naaman, Gehazzi and Uzziah who subsequently turned leprous-white, implying that their skin was not white at all before they were cursed (Numb 12:1-15; 2 Kings 5: 1-27; 15:5).

While race and culture plays a major role in linking any people with their past so as to proceed knowledgeably into the future, the history of one's race and culture can not by themselves suffice to authenticate one's self. The Bible is therefore the most authentic textbook to be used to reveal the identity of each tribe and race on earth. The Bible truly is the primary source for legitimate identity as it fulfils this function without prejudice or bias. There is however enough room for archeology to satisfy the desire to know the actual location of a site mentioned in the Bible. In this case when all the research data agree, all including the

Biblical evidence and the extra-Biblical documents then the basis to establish the truth would have been fully laid down.

For instance, there is no trace of the ancient name, Megiddo, but the location is certain and was confirmed beyond doubt by excavation. Sometimes the text of the Bible does not provide enough information about the location of a town, then it is the prerogative of the geographer to research elsewhere, in documents contemporary with, or later than the biblical account. One very important work is that of Egyptian Pharaohs who recorded lists of captured towns, diligently compiled by chroniclers who accompanied these Pharaohs of the new empire on their expeditions. Thothmes 111 listed one hundred and eighteen Canaanite towns which he conquered. These records were carved three times over, in the temples of Karnak. On the other hand Rameses 11 also had a somewhat similar record on the base of his own statue at Luxor. Pharaoh Shishak recorded one hundred and fifty six Israelite cities which he conquered during his famous campaign against Judah (1Kings 14:25).

Assyrian conquerors were also accompanied by trained scribes for the same purpose. Much information can also be found in archives of cuneiform tablets, commemorative stelae, fragments of ancient records of travels and historical descriptions, and geographical treatises by authors. The Jewish writer Flavious Josephus (*ca* A.D. 37-100) deserves mention here. He lived more than thirty five years in Palestine, taking a keen interest in the history of the country and its people, and in the exercise of his military and political duties was able to bring together in his works a great deal of geographical information.

CHAPTER ONE

AFRICA'S UPWARD CONNECTION

A study of races rooted in the Bible links the understanding of such a people with an eternal purpose. Blacks, according to scripture, are a result of God's love and grace. The fact that the very lineage of Jesus Christ includes Blacks and that the leadership of the first century church included Africans indicates that Africans are an integral part of God's redemptive master plan.

THE GREAT CIVILISATIONS

Indigenous humanity and the originators of the civilizations in both Mesopotamia and Africa were Blacks. They truly were Black in Asia's Lower Mesopotamia and they were Black in Africa. Either way one may cut it the originators of the world civilizations were Blacks or Black people. The Historian Lerone Bennett concludes this by saying;

> Civilizations started in the great river valleys of Africa and Asia, in the Fertile Crescent in the Near East and along the narrow ribbon of the Nile. In the Nile Valley that beginning was an African as well as an Asian achievement. Blacks, or people who would be considered Black today, were among the first people to use tools, paint pictures, plant seeds and worship gods (Before the Mayflower. 1982, p.5).

It is true that civilization dawned in the region between the two major rivers of Tigris and Euphrates. There is a fertile and broad valley between Tigris and Euphrates rivers known to the Greeks as the Mesopotamia, which means 'the land between the two rivers'. In the Southern parts of this long valley an energetic and inventive people began to construct the world's first cities. They invented a system of writing (other than hieroglyphics which the Egyptians invented) and were the first also to use wheeled vehicles.

Mesopotamian people survived for more than three thousand years until the conquest of Babylon by the Persians in 539 B.C. This made it even part of a wider empire.

UR' OF CHALDEANS-A HIGHLY CULTURED AND SOPHISTICATED ANCIENT CITY.

The Chaldean city, Ur, which was located south of Mesopotamia and southeast of Babylon was inhabited by the dark-skinned Semites. The Negro Babylonians and

Chaldeans for centuries intermixed, and because of this, became one in race, language and civilization. Being the father of the Hebrews, Abram's ancestral roots are traced from the city of Ur (Gen 11:28; 15:7; Neh 9:7; 1Chron 11:35){The Encyclopedia Britannica, Vol 8. 1959, and The New Funk and Wagnalls Encyclopedia, Vol. XII. P 4199-4200}.

At the beginning of the second millennium B.C., when Abram lived there, the city possessed an exceptionally high culture. Houses were constructed, and usually two stories high. Rooms on the ground floor were grouped around a central courtyard, and a staircase led up to the second story. The city had an efficient sewage system which is more than some cities in that country can boast even today (The S.D.A. Bible Commentary Vol. 1.1953, p.290).

The Impact of the Spade

Archaeology and anthropology have played a great role in unearthing gems of truth that had long been either misrepresented or forgotten. In Syria, at Ebla, there was such a research which finally revealed the following findings which were written on a tablet of stone;

- Contains common names of biblical characters of Noah, Jonah, David, Adam and Eve.

- Contains also much detail needful to our book, such like the origin of Ham the father of Africans.

- That the world's oldest bones, weapons, tools, utensils and civilizations are found in Africa.

EGYPT IN AFRICA

The most spectacular monuments left by people of the ancient world were the work of civilization which took root in the narrow seed-bed of the Nile Valley and blossomed for the astonishing span of three thousand five hundred years. This legacy of Egypt includes the Pyramids of Giza, The Great Sphinx and the treasure of the boy king, King Tutankhamun. The other remarkable feature which lies in the Cairo Museum are the mummies of great rulers of ancient Egypt. A visitor can have the privilege of gazing at the faces of kings who died two thousand years before Christopher Columbus and his team carried the European civilization to the Americas.

Birthplace of Written Records

In a temple at Nekhen was found a two feet high palette whose records dates from 3100 B.C. According to historians, this is the world's earliest historical record, and the earliest example of the Egyptians' Hieroglyphic Writing. Yes, as mentioned before, the idea of writing may have its roots in Mesopotamia, but the *hieroglyphic* system which employs pictorial writing to communicate ideas and sounds originated in Egypt. This system is entirely different from the Sumerian cuneiform script. The earliest forms of Egyptian hieroglyphics are historical records whereas the Mesopotamian cuneiform script are economic texts.

Making of the Earliest Nation

By about 3400 B.C. Egypt had two main kingdoms. Upper Egypt was governed from Nekhen, a town about sixty kilometers south of Luxor. Lower Egypt was governed from the region of The Nile Delta. This status-quo was disrupted by Menes, the King of Nekhen who conquered and became the first king of Upper and Lower Egypt in about 3200B.C. This man was the first in a long line of Pharaohs whose name was preserved in the temple records. The word 'pharaoh' means 'palace 'or 'Great House' according to Egyptian understanding.

Through Menes and his successors, Egyptians became the very first people to achieve nationhood in a world where small principalities and city states were the normal pattern of society.

Discovery of Papyrus

As writing progressed on into complex and more developed scripts the Egyptians then discovered a new surface far more superior to the clay tablets of Mesopotamia, this was the papyrus. This was a plant whose pith was cut into strips of equal length and then placed side by side. These would then be beaten flat to produce smooth sheets on which scribes wrote in ink. Papyrus is the origin of the English word 'paper'.

The Calendar, Mathematics and Medicine

The Egyptians evolved a system of mathematics so as to deal with problems in the construction industry. This enabled scribes to work with fractions and square roots, to calculate the area of a circle and volume of a cylinder.

The Egyptians went ahead and named and mapped the stars. The three hundred and sixty five day calendar is believed to be a legacy from ancient Egyptians. They would date their year from the appearance of the star Sirius, just before the annual floods of the Nile River. This helped them to divide the year into twelve monthly segments.

Famous Doctors and Surgeons

From the preparation of a dead body for mummification, the Egyptians picked up the knowledge of human anatomy. To this effect, Egyptian doctors and surgeons were famous throughout the world. Experiments which also were carried out with healing properties of various African plants including the opium poppy gave Egyptian doctors an edge on sound understanding of medicines. According to Bertha Morris Parker, the earliest doctor was an Egyptian, Imhotep, who is said to have lived as long ago as 2980 B.C. (Fascinating Facts: A Treasure of Information on Hundreds of Subjects.1970, p. 9).

The *Shadoof*

The Egyptians were the first in Irrigation Systems as evidenced by the testimony of the *shadoof.* Archeologists found one *shadoof* in a tomb at Thebes. The weight of the water of a *shadoof* is balanced by a counterweight placed at the end of a long pole. When using a *shadoof,* one man can raise six hundred gallons of water in one single day.

Perfecting of Arts

When Greeks first visited Egypt they marveled at the already flourishing civilization; cities with their thronged streets, brightly painted and polished temples and pageantry.

Metal working techniques which originated in Mesopotamia were perfected in Egypt. Furniture, ornaments and many objects of daily usage were also perfected here. Opaque glass too, was perfected by Egyptian craftsmen.

African Aeronautics

The Africans were drawing and flying airships some good two thousand years before Da Vinci's idea of flying, and some three thousand years before the Wright Brothers even had a slight thought over possibilities of travelling above the ground level. The Ethiopians had developed airships that could fly for some few hundred feet above the ground. History has it that in 1922, a model of sailplane was found in the tomb of King Tut. In 1969 Dr. Khalil Missiha(who studies birds), while looking through a box of bird models in a Cairo Museum Storeroom, was startled to discover a two thousand year old model of an airplane, made of sycamore wood. It looked modernistic and resembled the American Hercules Transport aircraft.

Hair Saloons

Some four thousand years ago, The Blacks of ancient Egypt, long before propagating with Europeans, used hot comps made from iron to press their thick, wooly, peppercorn hair, over. Blacks also excelled in the field of cosmetics. To this effect the record says that the first head of hair to ever exist, was Negro wool hair.

ANCIENT HAMITICS

The ancient Hamitics were known for their strength and courage. Herodotus reported that while visiting Africa, he saw some of the blackest and tallest men of all men on earth. The record in Isaiah 45:14 also states that the Negro Serbians, who were descendants of Seba through Cush were tall men. The great researcher, G. D. Kittler submits to the fact that The Watusi of Africa is the tallest race in the world, whose members can reach the height of seven to eight feet (Let's Travel in the Congo. 1965, p.30).

On the other hand most historians who include Hawkes, Wooly and Pliny say that Negroes are among the tallest of all humans. "The Ethiopians were over eight cubits in height", says Pliny (Naturalis Historia, p. 23-79). Another historian, Linton concludes it by saying, "Negroes are the tallest and the shortest of the human breed" (The Study of Men. p. 41). Intermarriage between Africans (Hamitics) and Hebrews (Semites) became one reason why Ham's stature could not remain as gigantic as before.

Frank M. Snowden writes of a black huntsman called Olympius whom he describes as a Herculean whose name was synonymous to success. He had innumerable victories recorded in ancient history books. The Great Negro Pugilist Nicaeus, nicknamed *The Brown Bomber of Antiquity*, with his swiftness and daring astounded the Roman Empire as he won fame throughout the ancient world.

The Negro Hittite

The Negro Hittites were described on the Egyptian and Assyrian Monuments as a great race of The North, whose shrewd army was feared for its valor and size. This army was much capable of coping with Assyria, Egypt and any other earthly power at war. (Culture and History of the Black Experience "September 1974 issue" of 'The Message Magazine' p.6).

The Hamitic Hittites were a sturdy race whose men were pictured as beardless (Gen 10:6; 1 Sam 26:6-7).

THE LATER YEARS

In 1798. A.D. when the French under Napoleon plundered Egypt, Europe became highly astonished to learn that the Ethiopians and Egyptians whom they had thought to be inferior were actually the originators of the world's first powers. Through archaeology and recorded findings the French had reluctantly unmasked a hidden civilization of two Negro elements which for centuries past had led the world culturally in many facets. Without question, Napoleon's expedition had disclosed a long buried secret about Africa and her gift to the world. European and American scholars, philosophers and the like, then dropped Europe and accepted Africa and the Near East as the cradle of life and civilization. They had learnt a new lesson that the Western Civilization was a borrowed culture from the Negroes ; that great thinkers such as Socrates, Aristotle and Plato had learnt much from Africa ; and finally that The Negroes were once world dominators while Asia and Europe were relatively uncivilized(The Black Biblical Heritage.1994, p. 238).

Hidden Identities

John L. Johnson writes the following in his exposition;

> From the beginning of time, the sons of Ham have heavily penetrated Europe thereby leaving a dosage of African blood. They mutated such nations like Portugal, Spain, Italy and other European lands from white blue-eyed blonds to darkish skinned,

brown-eyed coiled-curly haired heads. On the other hand J.P. Widney confirms that the Ancient Negroes who largely occupied Africa once settled a much broader area and rendered more authority globally than modern Negroes. J Hawkes and Sir L. Woolley say that the Negroids left a scattered trail eastwards from Africa to Southeast India and across the Indian Ocean to the Philippines, Australia, New Guinea, Melanesia and Tasmania (The Black Biblical Heritage. 1994, p. 237.

Archeologists confirm this position adding that ancient Negro remains can be found from Africa to Fiji Islands, China, Japan, Mexico, South America, Europe, Malaysia, etc).

DID YOU KNOW?

- At one time in history it was very difficult to distinguish between a Hebrew, an Egyptian, an Ethiopian and other African tribes if there was no birth record availed. In such cases the Hebrews were then known by their dialect, religion and dwelling place. Another famous historian, H. Norden says that he saw many Jews in Ethiopia who had kinky hair. The Bible also alludes to the same fact about Jews in Ethiopia(Amos 9:7; Zeph 3:10).

- The world's first empire after the flood was formulated and ruled by Ham's grandson, Nimrod. Nimrod means" brave".

- Of all nations mentioned in scripture, Ethiopia is mentioned first (Gen 2:12-13).

- The savior, Jesus' early childhood years were spent in Africa (Psa 68:31; Matt 2:13-15).

- The Gihon River which compasses Ethiopia from Eden is mentioned as being part of Adam's vicinity.

- The Pishon and Gihon Rivers were at one time associated with the Hiddekel and Euphrates River before the Global Deluge (The Global Flood of Noah's Time). Due to numerous volcanoes, floods, earthquakes over many years, there occurred a territorial change which separated these Rivers from Africa.

- Josephus, the great Jewish Historian together with many other historians have associated the Gihon River with the Nile. Also the word *Nile* is a Greek name translated from the Hebrew word *Gihon* (according to the Septuagint). The Greeks have always called the Nile River, *The River of Ham*.

CHAPTER TWO

THE AFRICAN GLORY SHINING THROUGH THE PAGES OF HISTORY

Hannibal with the African Elephants

Historians have it that during world conquests that were perpetuated then, Africa was always on the lead. The North African merchant State of Carthage had colonies of its own. It also had great wealth and a large fleet. Its founders were Hamitic Phoenicians. There were several European nations which fell under African dominance in history. Hannibal, the great "genius" Carthaginian General plundered deep into Europe, and seized Spain, Portugal, one portion of France and then made a triumphant trip across the Alps and subsequently conquered Rome.

When the Romans who were now great fighters by the year 264 B.C. tried to conquer Carthage, they felt they had finally met their match. For fifteen solid years (from 218 B.C. to 203 B.C.) Hannibal the Carthaginian Commander roamed up and down Italy after crossing over the Pyrenees and the Alps with his African Elephants. The Romans finally carried the war into Africa and attacked Carthage. The Carthaginians then recalled their commander, Hannibal so that he defends his nation, especially the capital. While on this errand Hannibal was attacked and defeated by the Roman General Scipio Africanus at Zama in the year 202 B.C. The Carthaginians became vassals to Rome up until 146 B.C. when the legions burnt it to the ground, ploughed over the site of the city and poured salt into all the furrows to make sure that the land remain forever infertile and barren (The Readers Digest History of Man. 1973, p. 70).

According to author John W. Weatherwax, modern canons, ship propellers, automatic hammers, flying missiles, gas motors, meat cleavers and even the upholstery tack hammers were developed in Africa's early use of power(The African Contribution, p 69).

> The great Roman historian, Pliny stated that about six thousand years ago mankind's brightest light of knowledge was developed on the continent of Africa. Africa was the centre set of civilization for some two thousand years before its rays of light streamed out of its shores into the remote nations of darkness. A pearl of knowledge including medicine, science, astronomy, art, architecture, military technique, agriculture and religion – which would bring forth, writing, the alphabet and the Bible - for centuries gave birth to

new civilizations such as ancient Israel, Persia, China, Greece, Rome, Scandinavia and the British Isles. This ancient light has risen throughout the history of man from the Stone Age to Modern Civilizations (The Black Biblical Heritage. 1994, p.15).

The prodigy of Africans can be traced in the pages of the Holy Writ. The prophet Nahum mentions them as follows, "Are you better than Thebes, situated on the Nile, with water around her? The river was her defense, the waters her wall. Cush and Egypt were her boundless strength, Put and Libya were among her allies"(Nahum 3:8,9).

The Hieroglyphics and the Alphabet

The word *alphabet* is derived from the first two letters in the Phoenician alphabet, *aleph* and *beth*. *Aleph* means ox and *beth* means house according to Phoenician understanding. This then was passed on to the Greeks as *alpha* and *beta*. The Phoenician letter *tau* was the same as T. Even where the letters have changed slightly over the centuries through their transmutations in Greek and Latin to modern Roman script, the derivation of the modern Western Alphabet is clearly from Phoenician. Inscriptions in this alphabetic writing which may date back to about 1300B.C. have been found in Byblos. Byblos was a Canaanite city found a little North of the modern Beirut. It was a hub of trade between the Semites and the Great Civilizations of Egypt.

Byblos date down to about 2600B.C. and is among the oldest and continuously inhabited towns in the whole world. It remained the most important city in the Eastern Mediterranean world for five hundred years up until it was eclipsed by Tire and Sidon.

Phoenician merchants also took with them papyrus to Greece and the Greeks coined the word *biblia*, from the town *Byblos* to describe the books made from it. Therefore, the English word 'Bible' comes from the Greek original, while the papyrus itself provide the word, 'paper'. It should also be noted that Phoenicians made textiles using wool from Mesopotamia and flax and linen from Egypt. From a shellfish called murex, the Phoenicians extracted a dye called the famous Tirian Purple. The finest and most expensive shade of this dye became the traditional color which denotes royalty, the purple color. It was from the Greek, *phoenix*, which means 'purple' that the Phoenicians derived their name.

CHAPTER THREE

AFRICA'S BIBLICAL LEGACY

African Origins

The Genesis record unequivocally brings us to the Noah and his family story. Ezekiel 29:10 mentions more than one river between Egypt and Ethiopia: this substantiates the Pishon River as an upper branch of the Nile River. Also Pliny, the Roman historian spoke of Havilah as in East Africa. The Bible also confirms thus: "A river watering the garden flowed from Eden; from there it was separated into four headwaters. The name of the first is the Pishon; it winds through the entire land of Havilah, where there is gold. The gold of that land is good; aromatic resin and onyx are also there. The name of the second river is the Gihon; it winds through the entire land of Cush" (Gen 2:10-13).

In Genesis 9 we see Noah's three sons Shem Ham and Japheth, the producers of all races upon planet earth, getting out of the ark. Because God confounded their language at the Tower of Babel (Gen 11:7), the children of Noah then began to scatter all over mother earth. Japheth, who became the father of the Caucasian race(Europeans) moved Northwards and settled North of the Mediterranean Sea. Shem and Ham moved Southeast and Southwest. Shem occupied the land which we call Syria today, Assyria, the Persian Gulf and some large parts of Arabia. Shem is the father of the Hebrews.

Now Ham, who had four sons (namely Kush, Mizraim, Put and Canaan) is the father of the African race. Cush was the progenitor of the Ethiopian people. This is validated by the fact that the names Cush and Ethiopia are used interchangeably in scripture(Gen 2:13;10;6). Mizraim was the progenitor of the Egyptians (Psa 78:51;105:23,26,27;106:21,22). Put was the Progenitor of the Libyans, while Canaan was the progenitor of the Canaanites. The Canaanites were notoriously idolatrous, a constant problematic snare to God's chosen people, the Hebrews.

In Gen Chapter 2:11, Africa is the continent to be first and foremost recorded in the Holy Bible before any other continent is mentioned. The name Havilla is the same as Cush or Ethiopia (Gen 10:6-7; Psa 105:23-27; 106:19-23).

The Bible was put here for the human race, yet ninety percent of the stories and events recorded in the Bible are about the children of Ham (i.e. Negroes or Blacks) and Shem (Hebrews or Semitics). Such names like Ai, Beersheba, Gilgal, Hebron, Jericho, Jerusalem, Joppa

Kedesh, Mamre, Salem, Sidon and Tire were originated and used by the Negroes. The Hebrews thereby later adopted these names(Psa 105:23-27;106:21-22).

It should be noted that the words mulatto and creole, are usually used to avoid the use of the word, Negro. During the early 600s A.D. the term "moor" which meant people with black faces, was most commonly used in Europe to refer to Africans/ Hamitics.

The Hamitics and Hebrews dwelt together for centuries. This resulted in many mixed marriages between the two tribes(Ezra 9:12;10:14,16-19;Gen 34:2,9,16,21;Num 31:9). Many Hamitics were overlooked in the Bible because they adopted Hebrew names and were subsequently called Israelites for they were born there. This is the same scenario in Russia,, Spain, America etc., where some natives can be traced back to Ham (Gen 10:6-20; 1Chronicles 1:8-13).

Melanin

This is a body chemical that produces black, dark and brown skin colors so as to absorb the rays of the sun in order to endure tropical life. It is a prehistoric substance that is found amongst about eighty five percent of people on planet earth. It is found among Africans, Asians, South and Central Americans, North American Blacks and Indians, Australian Aborigines (this is a Negro race in Australia), Melanesians (i.e., Black Islanders), Tasmanians, etc. Mixed breeding has reduced the amount of melanin in Negroes of the Western Hemisphere and Europe.

According to the Readers' Digest History of Man, 1973, the typical Semites (Hebrews), like most East Mediterranean peoples to this day had dark hair and olive skins.

DID YOU KNOW?

- Some of the Original Asians were a product of Ham. The Greek historian, Herodotus spoke of African and Asian Ethiopians. Professor Munro, a leading authority on Japanese life and culture says that the people of Japan are a mixture of Negro. Their flat nose, prognathism and brachycephaly, says Munro, could be traced to the Negro.

- The color black from ancient times has been associated with power, justice and wisdom(Deut 5:22).

- Some of the finest judicial systems the world over dress their men of justice in black: The nine justices of the twentieth century U.S. Supreme Court wear black robes. Many priests, ministers and scholars address their congregations wearing black robes.

- Black robes are also worn at many college graduations

- Most heads of state, while motorcading among large populations prefer to be seen in black limousines; this distinguishes high position, honor and order.

- Surprisingly in Gen 15:12-13 God Himself chose to visit the Patriarch Abraham in the form of great blackness.

- The Hebrews normally heard Jehovah's voice descending through thick dark clouds(Deut 4:11-25;5:22-23).

- David says that as God descended from above, he made darkness his secret place...(Psa18:11;97:2).

Adam and Eve

Adam and Eve, contrary to many artists' impressions (depicting them as white- skinned), could not have been white-skinned. Considering the geographical region which they were created, should easily help to eliminate this fantasy. Yes, one author, Ellen G. White mentions that Adam was ruddy in complexion. Ruddy is a color from red earth: It is a blend of brownish-black and reddish-brown. "Adam" is a Hebrew term which means *red earth*. The Judaic Encyclopedia, also states that "Adamatu" means *dark red earth*. A closer look at the Red Indians today brings a depiction of somewhat blend of redness and blackness.

Frank Snowden Jr. mentions the Greek philostratus as describing Memmon as a black – skinned red- looking man. The Greek Statius agreed by talking of red Negroes with copper – colored skin. To this effect M. J. Hershovits says he saw African Negroes who varied in complexion, from brownish – black to reddish – brown, and Snowden mentions the Ethiopian Lycoris as being black as the mulberry: this is a dark purplish-red color(The Black Biblical Heritage. 1994, p.234).

In Jer 43:7 reference is made to the place called Tahpanhes which means "Palace of the Negro". The name Ham means 'hot' or 'heat' which is associated with burnt skin or dark skin color. One other example of naming conventions is the case of Simeon, called Niger(Acts 13;1). The Greek- English Lexicon of the New Testament comments, "Niger(dark complexioned), surname of Simeon the prophet".

Kedar means 'to be dark' (Gen 25:13; Psa120:5). Phinehas the Negro or Nubian (a dark-skinned people; Exo 6:25).

FOR THE RECORD

According to the Cambridge Encyclopedia Coin Collection Company a record exists that states that, in the year 705 A.D., there was a gold coin of Jesus Christ on the face and Emperor Justinian 11 on the reverse side. This coin got much publicity as it was being circulated throughout Byzantine. Of great interest is the fact that the full face bust of Justinian showed him to have had straight hair, while the full -face bust of Christ revealed wooly hair. This coin generated much interest especially on the race of Jesus Christ. Finally there arose a war of ownership of the same coin between the Byzantine and one neighboring nation.

Caucasus

The Caucasus Mountains are located within Europe and Asia, between the Black Sea and the Caspian Sea. Caucasus was etymologically derived from Japheth, Noah's eldest son. Japheth's race is called the Caucasian race.

The Translation of the word BLACK in other various languages

The following tongues translate **black** as listed below;

Arabic	Sudan/Akhal
Chinese	Hei
Czechoslovakian	Cerny
Danish	Sort
Dutch	Swart
Egyptian	Kem
Finnish	Musta
French	Noir
German	Schwarthy/Moor

Greek ....Ethiopian/Apay

Hungarian..Fekete

Italian ....Nero

Japanese ....Kuroi

Latin ....Nigrus/Nigrum

Norwegian ....Svart

Polish ....Czarny

Portugese..Nego/Preto

Rumanian ....Negru

Spanish ....Negro

Swahili ....Giza/Susi

Swedish...Svart

Turkish...Siyah

Vietnamese..Den

Yiddish...Shuahrts

Hebrew ....Ham/Kam

CHAPTER FOUR

AFRICAN PARTICIPATION IN THE BUILDING OF THE CHOSEN NATION- ISRAEL

Throughout The Old Testament history, Ham's descendants,(through God's providence) featured in a great deal to contribute to the wellbeing of the nation of Israel. The following list testifies to the same facts:

- Joseph's wife, Asenath who was an Ethiopian woman (daughter of Patipherah of Egypt) begat important leaders in the history of Israel, Ephraim and Manasseh (Gen 41:50-52).

- Jethro, the father in- law to Moses who gave us great insights on good governance and sound leadership principles was an Ethiopian from Median(Exodus 18;13-27).

- Zipporah, who married Moses the prophet of Israel was the daughter of Jethro, a priest from a Median tribe.

- Hobab, was the son to Jethro/Raquel, the same Median Priest. His major role was to act as chief scout as Israel journeyed from Egypt to Canaan through the trying treacherous wilderness(Num 10;29-33).

- Bathsheba, who bore King Solomon, the son of King David was also a descendant of Ham. This also may explain why Solomon had tanned skin with bushy black hair (Song of Solomon 5:10,11).

- Hiram, who displayed architectural skill in designing palaces and temples at King Solomon's request (also supplied lumber/cedar poles for the Lord's Temple) was a black king.

- Ebed-Melech, who was probably one of King Zedekiah's advisors facilitated the release of the prophet Jeremiah from a dungeon cell. This man was an Ethiopian eunuch(Jer 38:7-13; 39:15 – 18).

- There were also many Ethiopian Priests living in Judah around 899 B.C. The record states that for many centuries Ethiopians believed in Judaism and the coming of the Messiah while Europe was still deep in the dips of paganism. Soon after the crucifixion of Jesus many Ethiopians broke away from Judaism to serve Christ. Therefore, the children of Ham (Africans) recognized Israel's God way before the children of Japheth(Europeans). In the early church the Bible records clearly that it was the Africans who spread Christianity to the Greeks (Acts 11:20).

- To this effect Ellen G White comments that in regions beyond the sovereignty of Rome, there existed for hundreds of years masses of Christians who remained nearly entirely free from Papal corruption. They were surrounded by paganism, but continued to acknowledge the Bible as the sole authority of faith and held firmly to many of its truths. These followers of Christ believed in the continuity of the law of God and observed the Sabbath of the fourth commandment. Churches that held to this faith and practice existed in Central Africa and among the Armenians of Asia (The Great Controversy. 1888, p. 63).

- Cushi, David's servant was named after his country, Cushi. He was a foreigner serving in David's army under the commander Joab. After the death of Absalom, the son of David it was Cushi who was sent with the message to King David to convey this very important message (2 Sam 18:21-32). Cushi had such vital skills needed at the kings palace.

CUSHI: ETHIOPIA

The Greek Herodotus and Homer both confirm that Ethiopians were remote and their empires were extraordinarily wide places "where the sun never set". Diodorus praised the Ethiopians who dominated Meroe (Sudanese capital) and the adjacent land of Egypt. He regarded Ethiopians as the founding fathers of the Egyptian civilization. Lucian tells us that the Ethiopians were discoverers of astrology and that their popularity for wisdom was great, as they were in all aspects more prudent than other men. Herodotus called the Cushites, or Ethiopians, the most handsome people on earth. Pseudo-Callisthenes announced a Black Queen of Ethiopia during Alexander's era to be of wondrous beauty (The Black Biblical Heritage. 1994, p. 252).

There were several black officers serving in David's army and thousands of warriors who helped Israel's army to conquer neighboring armies. Also in the ancient world Israel and Africa enjoyed a steady political relationship between themselves. Much of Israel's rudiments of war and governance were borrowed from" Ham" Africa. For instance Moses whose vast knowledge of social, political and natural sciences of Egypt were learnt on Hamitic soils and later passed on to the Semitic people, the Israelites (Acts 7;22).

History has it that some two hundred years before Abraham the Negro Ethiopians had already developed a giant civilization. Also, the Negro Egyptians who learnt much of their civilization from their southern cousins, the Ethiopians, were at the height of their glory when the Hebrews chose to reside in Egypt (Gen 45:17-20;46:5-6;47:1,11,27). The great author, E. Ullendorff, in his book, *Ethiopia and the Bible* states that due to the Ethiopian Eunuch's involvement in religion Ethiopia became a Christian nation before Europe. The British writer C. F. Rey also concurs with Ullendorff when he states in his book," Unconquered Abyssinia" that Ethiopia was already practicing Christianity while the rest of Europe was still worshipping idol gods such as Thor and Odin (Acts 17:23; 1 Thess 1:9). Finally one of the American writers J.H. Shaw, in his book, *Ethiopia,* points out that Ethiopia had already instituted Christian Churches throughout its land long before William the Conqueror set foot on England soil, and a thousand years before Christopher Columbus discovered the 'New World'.

The Queen of Sheba: "Oath"

This lady who earned recognition by the Messiah, Jesus Christ as "Queen of the South" (Matt 12:42), was an Ethiopian by blood, land and culture. The Arabian writer Hamdan who lived during the tenth century states that the queen of Sheba's mother was an Ethiopian named Ekeye. The queen's quest for Knowledge actuated her to spend a fortune and much time to travel from Yemen to Jerusalem to see and know the truth by herself. She is also noted by the remark which she finally uttered as she saw the truth and was satisfied thereby: "The half was not told me", became a famous statement of her confession (c.f. Isaiah 60:6; Ezekiel 27:2-23;1Kings 10:1-13 and Gen 10:7).

The pen of inspiration by the prophet Isaiah also confirms the fame of Africa in the history of nations, "This is what the Lord says: 'The products of Egypt and the merchandise of Cush, and those tall Sabeans- they will come over to you and will be yours'; (Isaiah 45:14).

"At that time gifts will be brought to the Lord Almighty from a people tall and smooth – skinned, from a people feared far and wide, an aggressive nation of strange speech, whose land is divided by rivers" (Isaiah 18:7).

Blacks were always among the chosen Hebrew nation. For instance, Abraham married Ketura, Esau married black Judith and Bashemath (Gen 26:34 – 35; 27:46; 28:9). David married the Cushite Bathsheba while Moses also married Ziporrah from Ham's tribe.

AFRICANS IN LEADERSHIP POSITIONS OF THE EARLY CHRISTIAN CHURCH

The Early Christian Church was composed of many nations, and the record of Acts 13:1-3 is clear in revealing the fact that at Antioch, Simeon and Lucius were in the leadership of this Early Christian Church. The same were Africans.

- Simon of Cyrene who carried the cross of Christ Jesus was also from Africa(Mat 27:32).

-   Four of the several women mention in Matthew's genealogy of Jesus are of Hamitic descent as follows ; Tamar, Rahab Ruth and Bathsheba (Mat 1:1-16).

Whatever greatness is resident in the nations that find their roots in the sons of Ham must find the heritage of that greatness in God. Conversely those aspects of culture that stand against the character and revelation of God must be condemned.

For instance Nimrod, the descendant of Cush was a mighty ruler in Shinar. He finally became the father of the Assyrians and Babylonians. Nimrod's significance is that he was the first great leader of a world civilization (Gen 10:8,9). However in spite of all his glory, Nimrod led an international rebellion against God Almighty as he sought to establish a man-made one-world government in order to usurp God's rule. This of course became a clear beacon in the history of men when God swiftly responded by effecting decisive judgment to all races then existent.

CHAPTER FIVE

THE CURSE IN GENESIS CHAPTER NINE

In Gen 9: 25 we see Noah cursing Canaan, who was the son of Ham for the sins of the father. This was normal custom to the oriental societies. For instance when Solomon went against The Almighty God, by following other gods from the tribes of his numerous wives and concubines, God pronounced a punishment of tearing ten tribes from him. God however did not tear the kingdom during Solomon's reign, but his son Rehoboam suffered these dire consequences. This is the same principle Noah applied to this particular case.

The Canaanites moved (Gen12:5,6;9:18;10:15-19;Exo3:8; 1Chr1:40).

It was Canaan who was cursed, not Ham. Only one of Ham's four sons, not all four, was cursed. Therefore, all

Black people everywhere could not be cursed; they were not all cursed.

One thousand years after the curse on Canaan the first Negro and Canaanite nation to fall under the curse was Gibeon (Amorites and Hivites, Deut 7:11; Josh 9:2-3,7,15-16,21-27;10:1-12). Remember that although Africa was enslaved by the Western states, this was besides the results of the curse. The curse by Noah only applied to the Black Canaanites, not Black Africans (Gen 9:24-25).

Some historians state that by the year 1150 B.C. some sizeable number of Canaanites were pressed into the narrow coastal strip of the present –day Lebanon and became known as the Phoenicians. It is true that Israel failed to extirpate the Canaanites from the face of the earth but through mixed breeding with other nations and races the Canaanites as a race gradually lost their identity.

The curse made on Canaan finally found its most obvious fulfillment in the delayed, subjugation of Canaan (the promised land, land of milk and honey) by Israel through the generalship of Joshua, as he followed God's command (Josh 9:23;1 Kings 9:20-21).

It should be noted that the other three sons of Ham have continued as nations up to this very day because they were not cursed at all. These are Cush (Ethiopia, Mizraim (Egypt) and Put (Libya).

Another argument can be derived from the example of Isaac blessing Jacob. The narrative in Genesis chapter 27 is clear. It intimates that what God has blessed, no one can remove those blessings. "Isaac trembled violently and said, "Who was it then, that hunted game and brought it to me? I ate it just before you came and I blessed him- and indeed he will be blessed" Esau went further to request any reserved blessings which he also could not get because Jacob had received all and all the blessings.

We also see God blessing Noah and all his sons as follows, "Then God blessed Noah and his sons, saying to them, 'Be fruitful and increase in number and fill the earth….." (Genesis 9:1). Here it is also a point to note that if all the three sons of Noah were blessed by God, how come some say that Ham was cursed by Noah, his father? It is absurd to think that a father can curse his son who would have been blessed by his creator, God Himself. Another principle to remember is that, *what God has blessed, no one can curse.*

The Unfortunate Teachings and Myths

There is one myth that permeated Western Culture especially American culture; this is the myth that Africa was cursed by God. This further stated that due to the curse, Africans are spiritually inferior to Americans and Europeans alike. This was done for the following possible reasons;

- The European slave traders wanted to substantiate and justify their enslaving actions (The Portuguese and Spanish were the first Europeans to deal in the Black slave trade).

- The same enslavers wanted to instill an understanding of compliance in the minds of the slaves so that they would accept it as the normal state of affairs in the real world

- Puritans were attempting to turn America into "The City on a Hill" prophecy hence slavery would play an important role in fulfilling this notion. Slavery provided the much needed economic base for implementing this unfortunate theology.

- It would be doing God's will if slavery was perpetuated, and failing to do so would be going against God's will and therefore risk eternal damnation: The slaves were so indoctrinated into believing such ill-gotten theology to their unfortunate detriment.

Texts which were misapplied to benefit the slave masters are Gen 9:24-27; Eph 6:5;Col 3:22. Surprisingly the slave masters winked at the following texts which would counterbalance the equation;

- Philemon 1:16 ; "no longer as a slave but better than a slave, as a dear brother…but even dearer to you both as a man and as a brother in the Lord"

- 1 Cor 7:21 ; "For who was a slave when he was called by the Lord is the Lord's freedman, similarly he who was a free man when he was called is Christ's slave".

Dr William Banks summarizes the religious mentality behind slavery when he writes thus;

> The Portuguese and Spanish, the earliest slave traders rationalized that it was God's will to bring Black heathens into contact with Christianity even if it meant a lifetime of enforced servitude. Their ships carried slaves to labor in the Caribbean colonies as early as 1517. With the approval of their governments and the Roman Catholic Church, the sellers of flesh maintained that "Christianized" slaves were better off than free heathens.(The Black Church in the U.S. 1972, p.9).

Definitely this undertaking was from a person without proper knowledge of this previously unknown peoples of Africa. This became an American myth, that Africans did not know God and were therefore spiritually worse off than the Westerners. Let us have a glimpse of how the slave traders and masters treated their subjects as we look through the pen of sociologist Hank Allen;

> They came into slavery with varying languages, cultural traditions, rituals, and kinship networks. This alone with an unfamiliarity of American geography, effectively prevented slaves from effectively developing the kind of complex social organization, technology and mobilization that would be necessary to alleviate their plight. Moreover to reinforce their

brutal, social and psychological control, slave holders often eliminated any bonds of kinship or culture by dividing captured Africans into groups of mixed tribal origins before selling them to plantation owners(The Black Family: Its Unique Legacy, Current Challenges and Future Prospects, The Black Family: Past Present and Future. 1991, p.8).

The Evils of The Myth

It should be noted that the Black inferiority complex instilled in the past has had catastrophic consequences. Anthony T. Evans reiterates it this way;

This has hindered the church to be the salt and light in the social landscape of America. On the other hand the myth has kept the Black community from fully understanding and appreciating their own heritage and using it as a foundation for addressing the cataclysmic crisis the African-American community now faces. The myth has kept individuals hostage to the perspectives of their racial group, thus limiting personal development(Are Blacks Spiritually Inferior To Whites: The Dispelling of an American Myth. 1992, p.8,9).

The ills of the Black inferiority myth got to its peak when 'Dred Scott' s Decision' ruled that Black People (of America) were not legal persons, but rather property to be bought, sold, or killed at the whims of their masters.

Martin Luther King, Jr. said it well when he declared that no one can ride your back unless it is bent. The sad result of the inferiority myth is that the devil made sure that some Blacks themselves wished they were white. This then produced an evil path of self-destruction due to personal character ridicule within Black People. Dr. Evans also states that to worsen the matter, some church parishioners were allowed to breed slaves for both profit and pleasure (Are Blacks Spiritually Inferior to Whites? The Dispelling of an American Myth. 1992. p. 19).

In America alone, and among the Black community, there is high teenage pregnancy rate, a great number of fathers who do not consider it their responsibility to take care of the children they sire. There is an alarming rate of massive homicide of males between seventeen and twenty-five years at the hands of fellow Blacks. The Devil had well calculated the results. Blacks also make up fifty percent of the prison population in the ever crowded prison cells of America despite the fact that Black people constitute a mere twelve to thirteen percent of the country's population.

So you see how the Devil circumvents scripture just to suite his machination so as to ruin humanity using humanity. Ephesians 3:15 states that God the father is the source from whom every family in heaven and on earth derives its name. Peter also emphatically confessed in Acts 10:34,35; "I now realize how true it is that God does not show favoritism but accepts men from every nation who fear Him and do what is right".

CHAPTER SIX

THE ORIGINS OF CHRISTIANITY

It should be clearly noted that neither Christianity nor Judaism originated in Europe but in the Middle East. It was only through the promptings of the Holy Spirit that Europe obtained Christianity. Moreover the trend towards worshipping idols and the like is universal throughout humanity (c.f. Romans 1:21-23).

For instance the Book of Corinthians affirms this point as it states that Aphrodite was worshipped as one of the numerous deities of the day. She was the goddess of love and a temple was built in her honor, which housed one thousand prostitutes used as priestesses. So enraptured were the Corinthians with this vile practice that Aristophanes coined the word *korinthiazomai* meaning to commit fornication. Truly humanity without divinity breeds a creature of circumstances destined to the doldrums of oblivion.

Mexico

The Aztecs of Mexico were very barbaric in their idol worship styles and rituals. Since war had given them land and riches to the Aztecs every man had to offer human sacrifices to the numerous gods. It was human sacrifices more than anything else that appalled the few European visitors to Middle America. Human sacrifice had a long history in Mexico and was practiced by most of the tribes in Middle America. It is reported that when the temple of Huitzilopochtli was dedicated in 1487, as many as twenty thousand captives were sacrificed; one Cortez's companions counted 136,000 skulls which were on the rack that stood beside that temple in 1519.

Like all Middle American peoples, the Aztecs worshipped a multitude of gods and goddesses. It was believed that Huitzilopochtli, the national god of Aztecs was the son of a warrior god who was identified with the sun. Every night, it was believed that he would battle against the forces of darkness so that the sun would be reborn the next morning. Therefore man's duty was to provide nourishment in the form of human sacrifices, out of which the god demanded the blood and the human hearts. Captives taken in battle were taught that after death by this method they would go to paradise which they shared with those who had died in battle. To try to avoid this fate would be to disobey the will of gods. Legends praise prisoners who rejected all escaping opportunities and submitted to the knives. It was therefore reported that many victims went to the block to be slaughtered for sacrifice quite joyfully and willingly in anticipation of the so called special life in a special paradise, after death.

Rome

Roman religion was more of a state affair than a personal conscience, a ritual performed on behalf of the people by their priests in which the people themselves took no part. Roman towns had several temples dedicated to gods and goddesses representing different abstract concepts- Vesta for the hearth, Mars for military matters and warfare, and so on. New gods representing new concepts would be easily fitted into the system as the need arose. During a typical Roman ceremony the priest would offer a bull, a sow or a hen.

By the second century A.D. many foreign religions which were imported by traders and soldiers were being practiced as well. The Persian cult of Mithras, the Egyptian cult of Isis the mother goddess and Serapis her spouse and the Bacchic rites from Greece were some of the religions which were easily adopted. Christianity also entered the scene as an alternative religion offering a democratic after-life, offered great hope to the underprivileged and thus it was greatly embraced by women and slaves, during its early days. In the fourth Century A.D. Christianity was adopted as the official religion of Rome.

Let us look at some parts of Africa as we continue comparing and contrasting the barbaric nature with the civilizations of the ancient world as a whole.

Sudan

The drying up of the Sahara by 2000B.C had made the desert a formidable obstacle between the North and South. The trans-Saharan trade continued to brave the terrors of desert crossing. The ancient kingdom of Ghana arose in the eighth century and flourished for three hundred years. By the 13th century Mali had absorbed Ghana. When the Arab trader Leo Africanus visited Mali in the 16th Century he described its people to be superior to any other Negroes, in wit, civility and industry. The Sudanese kingdoms were from earliest times visited by Arab traders and explorers who converted the inhabitants to Islam. From Somali in the North to Mozambique in the South many little coastal states flourished. The island of Kilwa was the greatest medieval East African City. When Ibn Battuta, the great Muslim traveler visited Kilwa, in 1332, he described it as one of the most beautiful and best conducted towns he had ever seen.

From the lofty cool rooms of this cliff-top palace the rulers of Kilwa witnessed the arrival of gold from the South, and ivory from Lake Malawi. Much of the gold which made the eastern Coastal States rich came from the region of Zimbabwe. The granite ruins which still stand at Great Zimbabwe, of a palace on a hilltop and a temple in the valley below, are some of the most impressive remains of a great African civilization.

The first Europeans who saw the Great Zimbabwe stone ruins were Portuguese explorers seeking the legendary King Solomon's Mines. These then jumped to wild conclusions that these buildings were the works of South Arabians of the Queen of Sheba's time, or by Phoenicians. Research later revealed that the name Zimbabwe means 'Great Place of the King' (Dzimbahwe), or houses of stones, (Dzimba dzamahwe) and these ruins were the great achievements of a succession of a Bantu- Speaking African People, and the ancestors of the majority of Zimbabweans today. These buildings which were made of well-hewn stone were skillfully built without motor.

By the 15th Century Zimbabwe was an established and prosperous centre, perhaps the capital of a great empire, The Munhumutapa Empire. As per record Munhumutapa gold reached the Muslim world via the Zambezi Valley, and up to Sofala and Kilwa.

Interestingly, the Munhumutapa ruler was a religious king. His subjects approached him prone on their stomachs. The ordinary people, while they could hear his voice as he spoke were never allowed to see King Munhumutapa. The courtiers were supposed to imitate every action of the king: if he coughed, they would also cough, and if he sneezed, they would also sneeze. When King Munhumutapa became very sick or very old he had to induce self-inflicted death by taking poison.

After the Munhumutapa dynasty, the Rozvi were the most remarkable Dynasty in Zimbabwean history. During such dynasties Christianity then came to Zimbabwe in the late nineteenth Century.

THE MISSIONARY MOVEMENT

After the European Slave Trade had ended the Europeans came to Africa with a new set of motives;

- To open up the continent for trade

- To free the natives from Arab traders

- To bring Christianity to the continent

Therefore the first glimpse of the continent's vast commercial opportunities started a "Scramble for Africa" in the 1870s. Within thirty years the whole continent of the children of Ham was under European control except for Ethiopia and Liberia. Yes, Christianity also penetrated Africa: however in many places it has taken African forms whose emphasis is singing and some dancing which have always accompanied every important African ceremony/occasion.

When Europeans came to Africa, they had the idea that Africans understood little, if anything about God. They also had the idea that Africa had nothing to offer culturally and spiritually to the emerging civilizations of the West.

The Theological Link

Africans recognized God the creator through His invisible attributes, but not unto salvation because they did not know Jesus Christ (Rom1:19, 20). Africa did not have the gospel of salvation through the merits of Jesus Christ who shed His precious saving blood on the cross of Calvary. Instead Africans only understood God through sub- deities as means of access to God, the creator of the universe (*Musikavanhu*, *Nyadenga* or *Nyatene*).

Let us consider the irony of the matter here as we ponder upon why slavery was allowed and later banned.

Doctor Antony Evans clearly posits that slavery was permitted in Africa not so much to teach the savage the right way, but rather as in the case of Cornelius, to acknowledge the slave's faith in the true high God, by introducing him to Jesus Christ: Him being the only way to God, the only mediator and not any other sub deities. Secondly Dr. Evans points out that slavery was allowed thus as a means by which God would introduce the true meaning of His justice to America and Europe which had neglected this aspect of His character (Are Blacks Spiritually Inferior to Whites?: Dispelling of an American Myth. 1994).

Dr. Evans brings to light the story of Joseph as recorded in Gen 37-50. As Joseph endured untold havoc for the sake of an ultimate victory, so was the plight of the African slave. In his assessment of his ordeal Joseph said to his brothers, "As for you, you meant evil against me, but God meant it for good in order to bring about this present result, to preserve many people alive (Gen 50:20).

Pastor Gift Rwodzi, in his commentary on the book of Revelation, puts it this way;

Disobedience to God's will brings about evil consequences, and God blesses the nation where He is honored. The Scramble for Africa besides its ills has brought to Africa a blessing in disguise; for it also allowed missionaries to take advantage of the situation in order to bring true worship which leads to salvation through Jesus Christ (*Kuzarura Zvakazarurwa/* Unveiling Revelation. 2011 p.96,97).

During The Scramble for Africa Episode, there were notably two major groups of settlers who had different motives. The first group was after African wealth which they exploited and exported to their home countries. This group we can safely term "The A Team". The second group of settlers who followed the "A Team" were missionaries whose only motives were purely religious. For our purpose let us term them "The B Team". The London Missionary Society (L.M.S) is one very good example of such missionaries in this category. The only problem was that the Africans were overwhelmed by acts of the "A Team" so much that they failed to figure out the difference that existed between the two teams.

In some cases, the two teams co-existed side by side as "The B Team" needed the military protection from "The A Team". Despite the above scenario, God's purpose ultimately prevailed. However to the ordinary Africans the Devil magnified the atrocities so caused by him through the acts of the greedy "A Team" Settlers so much that the benefits of Christianity were almost unrecognized as they were so much relegated to the peripheries of the arena. Throughout all the history of Africa even to the time of the advent of those missionaries the devil would fight tooth and claw to discredit God in the minds of the beholders. No wonder why some Africans even today do not accept Jesus as their personal savior arguing that we were told about Him through the works of the White men, the settlers, whom we later fought as an enemy of Africa.

As soon as a nation had accepted Christ Jesus and the merits of the cross, God allowed that nation to receive its own independence. Yes God is there among the struggles of nations toward their independence (Daniel 4:32; 2:47, 21;4:17; Rev 17:14). It is true that the Devil is in the business of starting wars and national unrest and all sufferings but The Great God who created peace can stop them all at His own appointed time.

God Directs the Fate of Nations

African nations which took longer to appreciate God's mercy within their boarders would take longer to realize the desired independence and sovereignty. God really directs the fate of each nation since He is an interested party in the affairs of nations. The nation of Israel was under Egyptian bondage for up to four hundred and thirty years due to its disobedience toward God's commandments. During the long period of captivity, it appeared as though Egypt was correct in its misdeeds of slavery and that God was not even aware of the plight of the suffering Israelite nation. It came a time in 1445 B.C. when Heavens said enough is enough to Pharaoh and indeed Israelites were freed from national slavery with a mighty hand of the Almighty (Exo 13). Indeed the appointed time had come (Gal 4:4).

It should be clearly noted that God's ways are far removed from our ways and His understanding can not be comprehended fully by mortal beings; He is infinite and we are finite beings.

In the book, Miracles of Grace by Abraham J. Oberholster on p.46 we glean the following legend;

> The inhabitants of Iraq would never allow any doctrine of Christianity to be preached within their boarders. Then there was war between Iraq and Kuwait over oil fields. America intervened by sending troops of soldiers armed with their usual ammunition. However, one sinister ammunition given to each American soldier was a brand new copy of the Holy Bible so as to read when ever necessary. Before each soldier could have an opportunity to read the messages in the Holy Writ, the Iran Iraq War was over and America had to withdraw its troops. Providentially, all the Bibles were left in Iraq soil. Few months down the line, it is reported that Iraq sent an envoy to request a teacher from America to go to Iraq so as to educate them on the man Jesus, who was being referred to in the so many Bibles left by the American soldiers. Notably the Gulf Tanker War and many other wars by Arab countries necessitated the advent of Christianity in such nations which were much alienated to God, and Christianity.

Does God use evil ways to achieve His righteous goals? No, not at all. God in His omniscience and unfathomable wisdom "takes advantage" of existing situations in the normal and abnormal processes of human life, to reach His estranged sons and daughters. He wants us saved at all cost, for the ransom was paid at the cross in A.D. 31 upon Calvary's mountain; that is a great price.

It is like the story of the evils of Joseph's brothers and the ultimate blessings wrought by God for the same family. God only "capitalized" on the evil motives and actions then maneuvered His way to achieve His righteous intends. The Devil is on his errands of destruction and alienations day by day while God is in the business of propagating righteousness so as to save the nations from their sins. It seems as though the daily acts of the Devil are taking a successful swipe. True Christians may lose many life battles to the Devil, but the final War Results are in their (Christians) favor. I want to submit to you that it is the ultimate results of this struggle that counts. Christ ultimately triumphs in this warfare. History confirms this submission.

For instance, in the world's quest for riches many are exploiting all opportunities so as to amass much wealth. Avenues used are technological advancement such like the internet means of communication, fast transport, and treating the world as a small global village. These the nations are exploiting as means to achieve their selfish ends and thereby perpetuate evil and fulfill Satan's goals. God then directs His servants to utilize these opportunities to reach as many individuals as is possible so that salvation reaches all and sundry. The prophet Daniel was shown these things, that there will be great ease in travelling and communication, and the increase of knowledge (Daniel 12:4). Matthew also talks of the spread of this gospel of the kingdom to all nations, just before the end comes (Mat 24:14).

God's Ways Are Always Righteous.

Looking at the puzzle of national history, we realize that the freed Israelites were given land that the Canaanites thought was theirs in the first place. Canaan who was a descendant of Ham our great progenitor was never given that land by God but just occupied it through greed and disobedience. The disobedience of Canaan had reached its climax by the time Israel crossed the Red Sea toward Canaan, the Land which flowed with milk and honey. Canaan had indeed filled his cup of iniquity by the time God delivered Israel from Egyptian bondage.

To each of us God gives His Ten commandments which we ought to follow. Our individual attitudes towards such commandments determines our peace through God's protection and guidance or otherwise. Each person is the architect of his/her destiny through the choices made on a daily basis.

ALL NATIONS ARE BIDDEN TO
FOLLOW CHRIST TODAY

John 3:16 is clear in its invitation: "For God so loved the world that He gave His one and only son, that whosoever believes in Him shall not perish, but have eternal life".

In Revelation 7: 9-11, we are shown how that love of God and grace of Jesus Christ together with the works of the Holy Spirit achieve a massive harvest:

"After this I looked and there before me was a great multitude that no one could count, from every nation, tribe, people, and language, standing before the throne and front of the Lamb. They were wearing white robes and were holding palm branches in their hands. And they cried out in a loud voice: 'Salvation belongs to our God, who sits on the throne, and to the Lamb'"

Indeed, Africans are very much included in that statement, 'from every nation, tribe, people, and language'. There is therefore no reason why anyone must keep on referring to the curse of Genesis 9:25 as an excuse for failure to accept Christ and walk in His statutes. This is the only way to salvation, there is no any other way (Acts 4:12). God has reserved a place for everyone in His Master plan of Redemption, just believe, and you will be saved so as to be numbered with the great multitude which John was shown in that great vision.

CHAPTER SEVEN

DEPARTING OF THE AFRICAN GLORY (*ICHABOD*) AND THE RESTORATION

The Departing of the Glory

"Ichabod"

How is it that Negroes, who discovered science, engineering, medicine and the fine arts; these Negroes once living in the highest echelons of civilization, mastering the world's highest economy and diplomacy for thousands of years long before Europe, lost its grip on the same?

Africa has the second largest land area in the whole world continents. Its land area of 30, 330, 000 square kilometres is almost twenty two percent the world's total land area. If we put The united States of America into it, Europe into it, India, China, Argentina and New Zealand they all fit without any hassles. African land is very good and fertile for farming activities.

Mineral Resources.

The researches carried out in Africa reveal that the continent is highly laced with diamonds, with much gold, copper, bauxite, manganese, nickel, platinum, cobalt, radium and phosphates. Natural fuels and asbestos, iron and tin, chromium, lead, sulphur graphite and limestone are some of the riches found in the continent of Africa, our rich motherland. Some of the minerals are being discovered each passing moment. It appears Africa's resources, if properly managed can suffice to sustain all the nations of the world. No doubt, if properly managed, the resources of Africa can create enough employment for almost half the world's young people.

THE IRONY OF IT ALL

The questions that need to be attended to are these:

1. Why is Africa selling its natural resources to the world at very cheap prices only to buy them as finished products at exorbitant costs?

2. Why is African labour so cheap and yet this is the best asset an nation can ever posses?

3. Why is there much poverty in Africa yet this is the source of much world riches?

4. We have too much of disease outbreaks, too much of dehumanisation and injustices, too much of unfair labour practices and low incomes. Why? The paradox is clearly evident and these questions need answers today.

As many have tried to answer such pertinent questions we also want to indicate some factors from the book *What is Africa's Problem*, where the late Museveni of Uganda said, "One of the biggest weakening factors in Africa is tribalism and other forms of sectarianism…" while the late Samora Machel would say "tribalism is the commander-in-chief of anti-African forces"

In a further bid to answer some of the above questions Professor George Kinoti has identified nine causes which he outlined in his book, *Hope for Africa and What the Christian Can Do*. These are elaborated below:

1. Incompetent governments

2. Unjust international economic systems

3. Evil aspects of African Culture such as disregard for time

4. Poor management

5. Widespread illiteracy and educational standards

6. Immoral practices including tribalism, corruption, dishonesty and laziness

7.   Scientific and technological backwardness

8.   Population growth

9.   Man-made environmental crises

Let us also consider Chinua Achebe's cry for Africa.
He wrote in his book, *The Trouble with Nigeria*, and
said, "We have lost the twentieth Century, are we bent
on seeing that our children also lose the twenty-first?
God forbid!"

How is it that Africa, who was once the richest continent
on earth with vast resources now find itself in the twenty
first century reeling in the doldrums of poverty. After
having reached such astonishing dominance in world
history, what could have befallen Africa at a later date in
history so much that it has some of the most deplorable
ghettos and slums in the world; what caused the collapse?

Black supremacy existed through from the Biblical
architectural Nimrod to the historical military genius,
Hannibal. Documented historical records reveal that the
Black Supremacy waned immediately after the fall of
Hannibal.

Centuries later, Europe, North America and others
invaded Africa and enslaved many, besides exploiting
Africa's mineral resources. Alexander the Great was one
of the first Europeans (Japhites, Gen 10:1) to conquer
Egypt; that was in 332 B.C. Then came the European
dominance. The Longest European rule over Africa came

from Rome, which held Egypt for nearly seven centuries. While residing in Egypt, many Japhithes intermingled with the Hamitics. Today one can visit the British Library and see coins bearing the image of the mighty Hannibal of Africa wearing earrings.

The intermarriages are attributed to the Egyptians gradual loss of much of their bushy-thick fuzzy-wuzzy hair and deep black skin. This scenario also happened to many other Hamitic Negro nations, which were conquered and ruled then by the Japhithes.

REASON ONE

CORRUPTION AND INEFFICIENCY

By the year 1085 B.C., the Golden Age of the Egyptian Empire was past. No sooner had Ramesses 11 died than the Libyans from the Western Oasis and sea raiders from the North began to press in upon the boarders of Egypt. This was greatly allowed of God because the leaders and common inhabitants of Egypt had become very corrupt and so inefficient that a passerby could detect the weakness. Ramesses' successors tried their best to defend the country and protect it from invasion but it was in vain. Jehovah God had removed His protection. For about two hundred years, the Pharaohs struggled to keep their thrones amid civil strife and dwindling resources, but this was in vain.

In the eighth century B.C. a family of energetic Sudanese Kings from the region of Napata took control of Egypt.

These kings became emboldened by success and went to challenge the mighty Assyrian Army that was in Palestine. The results were very drastic as these were defeated. The Napatan Kings and subjects were then chased out of Egyptian soil down to the southern regions and the Assyrian troops occupied the city of Memphis. Assyria was however also at the verge of its collapse when it occupied Memphis hence their stay in power was short-lived. Egypt then later regained its independence under a new line of kings whose capital was Sais.

In 525 B.C., Cambyses, the Persian marched from Palestine and conquered Egypt, and Egypt became a Persian Empire. Two Centuries later, in 332 B.C., Alexander the Great, fresh from his triumphant expeditions in Asia Minor and Syria entered Egypt, and the last Persian governor who was in charge of Egypt then surrendered. Upon Alexander's death, one of his generals, Ptolemy who was born in Macedonia and brought up in Greece took over. Now, the worship of Isis and her child Horus spread widely. This is the same picture that we normally see on walls in homes with a hallow of light encircled round about the head of the mother, Isis. That light is the sun which was worshipped in Egypt. Most of us think that the same picture is of Mary and The child Jesus; unfortunately, it is Isis and Horus the gods of Egypt. Sun worship which the Romans also adopted from Egypt has also secretly crept into the churches of today. This and all the emotional cults of Egypt enjoyed great popularity in Greece and Rome.

Later, in the year 30 B.C., the Romans conquered Egypt and converted many to Christianity. It was the coming of Christianity that sounded the death-knell of old Egyptian idolatrous religion. The ancient temples then crumbled as the gods were neglected and denounced. The tombs and their inhabitants were forgotten. This was then the time when the idea of religious men withdrawing from the world to found monasteries for prayer and meditation was first developed and subsequently spread to Europe.

After three thousand five hundred years, the civilization of the Nile had finally succumbed. Only its language lives on up to this day, in the form of worship of the Christian or the Coptic Church in Egypt.

REASON TWO

IDOLATRY- BREACH OF THE SECOND AND THIRD COMMANDMENTS

PHARAOH IS AMUN- RE; PHARAOH IS GOD?

In Egypt there was worship of Isis and Horus, gods which were believed to be related to the sun. The whole land of Egypt and its people belonged to the gods, and in particular, to Horus, whom Pharaoh was believed to represent here on earth. The king pharaoh's function (it was believed) was to maintain the order of the universe, the movement of the heavenly bodies, the rotation of the seasons, the annual floods and the fall of the River Nile.

Pharaoh was so revered that he was believed to be the channel through which humanity made contact with the spiritual world. The king was therefore the high priest in every temple of all other god in the land as he would intercede with the gods on the people's behalf. The Pharaoh would proceed to intercede by performing the proper rites and making the required offerings.

It should be noted that Egypt had hundreds of gods, some of whom took the form of creatures, such as cows, bulls, lionesses, monkeys, crocodiles, etcetera. Some gods were believed to be cosmic forces; the sun, moon, stars and the sky. This multiplicity of gods came by when the country was unified. The state religion had to absorb all existing cults of the conquered territories. Most of these cults originated in the worship of primitive totems and sacred objects.

The most important and most wealthy of all the Egyptian gods was Amun (Amun- Re). Amun was the patron god of the city of Thebes, the capital of the vast empire. In Thebes there is a very massive temple of Amun, besides numerous other temples of Egyptian gods. The temple, which was a very huge edifice was begun in about 2000. B.C. and kept on being added to by successive pharaohs, all to the glory of a god, Amun. All these struggles and efforts were meant to eclipse Jehovah's sovereignty in that land. This was idolatry at its peak and therefore irked the creator God and provoked His anger.

"The king, or Pharaoh was at least in theory all powerful and the owner of all the land in Egypt. It was believed that he was all divine and that he and his ancestors in the spirit world influenced the fertility of the land. He was thus a central figure in the elaborate religious system with a complicated order of gods served by powerful priests" (The Growth in African Civilization: The making of modern Africa.—p.6).

REASON THREE

PRIDE

Let us check with Ezekiel 29 which brings us to what we may call misdirected glory on the part of Africans during their world supremacy period. "This is what the Sovereign Lord says : I am against you Pharaoh, king of Egypt, you great monster lying among your streams. You say the Nile is mine I made it for myself" (Eze 29:3)

The God who tolerates no rivals has defeated all the gods of Egypt and their worshippers (Psa 35:10;71:19;89:6;113:5; Isa 40:18,25;46:5;Micah 7:18).

It is therefore evident that civilization without worshipping the creator of all success and all civilization ultimately results in loss of status, loss of all material blessings and finally leads to abject poverty and destruction. Only by way of true repentance can such a people be restored to their former position, by the grace and power of God Almighty.

It is pride that caused King Nebuchadnezzar to become insane for seven years under God' s retribution. It is pride that caused Lucifer to be arrogantly disobedient and disoriented thereby leading to his loss of position and status in Heaven. These remain as a lesson beacons to us who live in the last days of earth's history.

REASON FOUR

ARROGANCE- "WHO IS THE LORD THAT I SHOULD OBEY HIM...?".

In Exodus chapter five we see one of the greatest weaknesses of a strong nation. In the discussion between Moses, Aaron and Pharaoh we get the most important reason why Africa lost out in this regard. "... This is what the Lord, the God of Israel, says: 'Let my people go, so that they may hold a festival to me in the desert.'

Pharaoh said, "Who is the Lord, that I should obey Him and let Israel go? I do not know the Lord, and I will not let Israel go"(Exo 5:1,2).

"... But Aaron's staff swallowed up their staffs. Yet Pharaoh's heart became hard and he would not listen to them, just as the Lord had said"(Exo7:12,13).

> Commenting on the fate that befell the African state, Ellen White had this to say; It was because the Israelites were so disposed to connect themselves with the heathen and imitate their idolatry that God had permitted them to go down to Egypt where the influence of Joseph was widely felt and where circumstances were favorable for them to remain a

distinct people. However, here also, during the later part of the Hebrews stay in Egypt there was gross idolatry and cruelty. This was of course Satan's other avenue to frustrate God's grand purpose by darkening the minds of the Israelites (*emphasis supplied*).

Thou the Egyptians had long rejected the knowledge of God, the Lord still gave them opportunity for repentance. In the days of Joseph, Egypt had been an asylum for Israel; God had been honored in the kindness shown His people; and now the long-suffering One, slow to anger and full of compassion gave each judgment time to do its work. The Egyptians cursed through the very objects they had worshiped had evidence of the power of Jehovah and all who would might submit to god and escape His judgments. The bigotry and stubbornness of the king resulted in spreading the knowledge of God and bringing many of the Egyptians to give themselves to His service (Patriarchs and Prophets, 1890, p. 332, 333).

'He will set fire on the temples of the gods of Egypt; he will burn their temples and take their gods captive.... There is the temple of the sun in Egypt, he will demolish the sacred pillars and will burn down the temples of the gods of Egypt"(Jer 43:12,13).

"Woe to the obstinate children, declares the Lord, to those who carry out plans that are not mine, forming an alliance but not by my Spirit, heaping sin upon sin; who go down to Egypt without consulting me, who look for help to Pharaoh's protection, to Egypt's shade for refuge.

But Pharaoh's protection will be to your shame, Egypt's shade will bring you disgrace. …The envoys carry their riches on donkeys' backs, their treasures on the humps of camels, to that unprofitable nation, to Egypt, whose help is utterly useless. Therefore I call her Rahab the Do-Nothing (Isa 30:1-3, 6b-7).

> "A sword will come against Egypt, and anguish will come upon Cush. When the slain fall in Egypt, her wealth will be carried away and her foundations torn down. Cush and Put, Lydia and all Arabia, Libya and the people of the covenant land will fall by the sword along with Egypt. This is what the Lord says, The allies of Egypt will fall and her proud strength will fail. From Migdol to Aswan, they will fall by the sword within her, declares the sovereign Lord. They will be desolate among desolate lands, and their cities will lie among ruined cities. Then they will know that I am the Lord, when I set fire to Egypt and all her helpers are crushed. On that day messengers will go out from me in ships to frighten Cush out of her complacency. Anguish will take hold of them on the day of Egypt's doom, for it is sure to come"(Ezek 30:4-9).

"I will dry up the streams of the Nile, and sell the land to evil men; by the hand of foreigners I will lay waste the land and everything in it. I the Lord have spoken.

This is what the Sovereign Lord says:

I will destroy the idols and put an end to the images in Memphis. No longer will there be a prince in Egypt, and I will spread fear throughout the land. I will lay waste Upper Egypt, set fire to Zoan and inflict punishment to Thebes. I will pour out my wrath on Pelusium, the stronghold of Egypt and cut off the hordes of Thebes. I will set fire to Egypt, Pelusium will wreath in agony. Thebes will be taken by storm; Memphis will be in constant distress. The young men of Heliopolis and Bubastis will fall by the sword, and the cities themselves will go into captivity. Dark will be the day at Tahpanhes, when I break the yoke of Egypt; there her proud strength will come to an end....So I will inflict punishment on Egypt and they will know that I am the Lord" (Ezek 30:12-18a, 19).

WARS IN AFRICA (Isaiah 19:2-20).

The following texts give us a glimpse of why some wars were permitted to be fought on African soils for many years on end, notably some such wars still linger in and around the continent of Africa. "An oracle concerning Egypt: See, the Lord rides on a swift cloud and is coming to Egypt. The idols of Egypt tremble before Him and the hearts of the Egyptians melt within them. I will stir up Egyptian against Egyptian- brother will fight against brother, neighbor against neighbor, city against city, kingdom against kingdom. The Egyptians will lose heart and I will bring their plans to nothing; they will consult the idols and the spirits of the dead, the mediums and the spiritists. I will hand the Egyptians over to the power of a cruel master, and a fierce king will rule over them, declares the Lord, the Lord Almighty.

The waters of the river will dry up and the riverbed will be parched and dry. The canals will stink; the streams of Egypt will dwindle and dry up. The reeds and rushes will wither, also the plans along the Nile at the mouth of the river. Every sown field along the Nile will become parched, will blow away and be no more. The fishermen will groan and lament, all who cast hooks into the Nile; those who throw nets on the water will pine away. Those who work with combed flax will despair, the weavers of fine linen will lose hope.

The workers in cloth will be dejected, and all the wage earners will be sick at heart. The officials of Zoan are nothing but fools; the wise counselors of Pharaoh give senseless advice. How can you say to Pharaoh,' I am one of the wise men, a disciple of the ancient kings'?

Where are your wise men now? Let them show you and make known what the Lord Almighty has planned against Egypt. The officials of Zoan have become fools, the leaders of Memphis are deceived; the cornerstones of her peoples have led Egypt astray. The Lord has poured into them a spirit of dizziness; they make Egypt stagger in all that she does, as a drunkard staggers around in his vomit.

There is nothing Egypt can do – head or tail, palm branch or reed. In that day the Egyptians will be like women. They will shudder with fear at the uplifted hand that the Lord Almighty raises against them. And the Lord of Judah will bring terror to the Egyptians; everyone to whom Judah is mentioned will be terrified because of what the Lord Almighty is planning against them.

In that day five cities in Egypt will speak the language of Canaan and swear allegiance to the Lord Almighty. One of them will be called the City of destruction. In that day there will be an alter to the Lord in the heart of Egypt, and a monument to the Lord at its boarder. It will be a sign and witness to the Lord Almighty in the land of Egypt. When they cry out to the lord because of their oppressors He will send them a savior and defender and he will rescue them"(Isaiah 19: 1-20).

We here learn a vital lesson of life that we all need to be wary about. All the success one might enjoy is from God even if it is very much not clear to that effect. Every good thing is from God as history has revealed. If we achieve success and exclude God from the picture by neglecting worshipping Him we definitely experience a short-lived success. Though it might appear to be a long and enjoyable time period without God, He could have sustained it, if we choose to walk with Him so as to make it longer than what we would have achieved on our own. It is true that if we neglect God even if He had given us great blessings in the past, we will ultimately lose that which once belonged to us, then it will be given to another of God's choice. We must not cry foul and blame God if such circumstances befall us.

This scenario is what happened to the children of Ham. Beginning with Nimrod, whose rebellion was great enough to summon Heaven to come down to assess the extent of the ill-fated Tower of Babel Project, followed by Nebuchadnezzar whose ninety feet high golden image was placed in the plain of Dura (in the province of Babylon) to be worshipped, and ending with the last generation of idolaters: the results always are drastic as God intervenes so as to disallow their progress. Some such success stories would be so much obliterated that they soon become extinct from the minds of men and annals of records.

OH YES! AFRICA HAD BEEN WARNED

So, to the people of Egypt and of all the nations connected with the powerful kingdom, God manifested Himself through Joseph. Why did the Lord choose to exalt Joseph so highly among the Egyptians? He might have provided some other way for the accomplishment of His purpose for the children of Jacob; but He designed to make Joseph a light and He placed him in the palace of the king, that the heavenly illumination might extend far and near. By his wisdom and justice, by the purity and benevolence of his daily life, by his devotion to the interests of the people—and that people, a nation of idolaters – Joseph was a representative of Christ. In their benefactor to whom Egypt turned with gratitude and praise, that heathen people were to behold the love of their Creator and Redeemer.

So in Moses, God also placed a light beside the throne of the earth's greatest kingdom, that all who would, might learn of the true and living God. And all this light was given to the Egyptians before the hand of God was stretched out over them in judgments (Patriarchs and Prophets. 1890, p. 368).

RESTORATION

The ways of the Lord are righteousness. He does not wish to see His children suffer deprivations forever.

So the Lord will make Himself known to the Egyptians, and in that day, they will acknowledge the Lord. They will worship with sacrifices and grain offerings; they will make vows to the Lord and keep them...He will strike them and heal them. They will turn to the Lord and He will respond to their pleas and heal them.

In that day there will be a highway from Egypt to Assyria. The Assyrians will go to Egypt, and the Egyptians to Assyria. The Egyptians and Assyrians will worship together. In that day Israel will be the third along with Egypt and Assyria, a blessing on the earth. The Lord Almighty will bless them saying, 'Blessed be Egypt my people, Assyria my handiwork, and Israel my inheritance'" (Isaiah 19;21-25).

SUMMON YOUR POWER, OH LORD, GOD

"Summon your power, O God, show us your strength, O God as you have done before. Because of your temple at Jerusalem kings will bring you gifts. Rebuke the beasts among the reeds, the herd of bulls among the calves of the nations. Humbled, may it bring bars of silver. Scatter the nations who delight in war. Envoys will come from Egypt; Cush will submit herself to God. Sing to God, O kingdoms of the earth, sing praise to the Lord, to him who rides the ancient skies above, who thunders with mighty voice" (Psalm 68:28-33).

GOD HAS DECIDED TO ASSEMBLE THE NATIONS

"Then will I purify the lips of the peoples, that all of them may call on the name of the Lord and serve Him shoulder to shoulder. From beyond the rivers of Cush my worshippers, my scattered people, will bring me offerings. On that day you will not be put to shame for all the wrongs you have done to me, because I will remove from this city those who rejoice in their pride. Never again will you be haughty on my holy hill. But I will leave within you the meek and humble, who trust in the name of the Lord.

At that time I will gather you; at that time I will bring you home. I will give you honor and praise among all the peoples of the earth when I restore your fortunes before your very eyes says the Lord"(Zeph3:9-12,20).

A HOUSE OF PRAYER FOR ALL NATIONS

"This is what the Lord says: maintain justice and do what is right for my salvation is close at hand and my righteousness will soon be revealed. Blessed is the man who does this, the man who hold it fast, who keeps the Sabbath without desecrating it, and keeps his hand from doing any evil. Let no foreigner who has bound himself to the Lord say 'The Lord will surely exclude me from His people.' And let not any eunuch complain, 'I am only a dry tree'. For this is what the Lord says, : To the eunuchs who keep my Sabbaths, who choose what pleases me and hold fast to my covenant – to them I will give within my temple and its walls a memorial and a name better than sons and daughters; I will give them an everlasting name that will not be cut off. And foreigners who bind themselves to the Lord to serve Him, to love the name of the Lord and to worship Him ; all who keep the Sabbath without desecrating it and who hold fast to my covenant- these I will bring to my holy mountain and give them joy in my house of prayer.

Their burnt offerings and sacrifices will be accepted on my altar; for my house will be called a house of prayer for all nations"(Isa 56: 1-7).

WHOSOEVER BELIEVES

"For God so loved the world that He gave His one and only son, that whosoever believes in Him shall not perish but have eternal life. For God did not send His son into the world to condemn the world, but to save the world through Him. Whoever believes in Him is not condemned, but whoever does not believe stands condemned already because he has not believed in the name of God's one and only son"(John 3:16-18).

OUR GOD SHALL NOT BE ANGRY FOREVER

"In that day the Root of Jesse will stand as a banner for the peoples; the nations will rally to Him, and His place of rest will be glorious. In that day, the Lord will reach out His hand a second time, to reclaim the remnant that is left of His people from Assyria, from Lower Egypt, from Cush, from Elam, from Babylonia from Hamath and from the islands of the sea" (Isaiah 11: 10-11).

"For God did not appoint us to suffer wrath but to receive salvation through our Lord Jesus Christ. Therefore encourage one another and build each other up just as in fact you are doing (1 Thessalonians 5:9,11).

GOD'S PURPOSE TRIUMPHS ULTIMATELY

One may look at this mystery of nations this way; God gave Noah three sons Shem Ham and Japheth. Each of them played a pivotal role in the puzzle of life in all its facets. There was a unique 'relay-like' race put before all of them so that they participate together in the great race of nations.

1. To Ham was given the blessed button of world civilizations as a starting point. To The children of Ham, the Black race, some six thousand years ago was given great knowledge as it became the centre set of civilization for some two thousand years in succession. Ham was given a pearl of knowledge which included medicine, science, astronomy, art, architecture, military technique, agriculture, and religion –which would bring forth writing, the alphabet and finally the Holy Bible. This Hamitic Relay Button of knowledge caused the ancient civilization light to shine throughout the history of mankind.

2. To Shem, was given the Button of "The Promise", which had a sevenfold structure, as follows;

    •   I will make you a great nation

    •   I will bless you

    •   I will make your name great

    •   You will be a blessing

    •   I will bless those who bless you

    •   Whoever curses you I will curse

    •   All peoples on earth will be blessed through you(Gen 12:1-3).

From thence Shem became the depository of God's truth to all the world. In the book of Luke we see the same testimony re-echoed by Simeon, the holy elder; "For my eyes have seen your salvation, which you have prepared in the sight of all people, a light for revelation to the Gentiles and for glory to your people, Israel" (Luke 2:30-32). "I will also make you a light for the Gentiles, that you may bring my salvation to the ends of the earth" (Isaiah 49:6(b)).

So through Shem God had planned that the whole world would be evangelized according to God's choice and foreknowledge; thus salvation will be accessed by *all* through the same channel. So God purposed in His master plan that salvation should come to all nations through the Jews, the children of Shem. Let us hear Christ speak to the Samaritan woman at the well alluding to the same theology; "You Samaritans worship what you do not know; we worship what we do know, *for salvation is from the Jews*" (John 4: 22).

Ellen G. White, the renowned author of the nineteenth century points out the following:

> God called Abraham and prospered and honored him; and the patriarch's fidelity was a light to the people in all the countries of his sojourn. Abraham did not shut himself away from the people around him. He maintained friendly relations with the kings of the surrounding nations, by some of whom he was treated with great respect. His integrity and unselfishness[sic], his valor and benevolence were representing the character of God. In Mesopotamia, in Canaan, in Egypt and even to the inhabitants of Sodom, the God

of Heaven was revealed through His representative (Patriarchs and Prophets. 1890, p368).

Ellen G. White also posits that if Israel had been faithful enough according to God's great master plan, Jerusalem was going to be the world centre of worship and evangelism, and all the nations would be converted through that system. Just as the people of Jericho confessed; "… I know that the Lord has given this land to you and that a great fear of you has fallen on us, so that all who live in this country are melting in fear because of you. We have heard how the Lord dried up the water of the Red Sea for you when you came out of Egypt, and what you did to Sihon and Og, the two kings of the Amorites, east of the Jordan, whom you completely destroyed. When we heard of it, our hearts melted and everyone's courage failed because of you, for the Lord your God is God in Heaven above and on the earth below" (Joshua 2: 9-11).

In the deliverance of Israel from Egypt, the knowledge of the power of God spread far an wide; even the warlike people of Jericho trembled. Centuries after this exodus the priests of the Philistines reminded their people of the plagues of Egypt and warned them against resisting the God of Israel (Patriarchs and Prophets, 1890, p 369).

3. To Japheth was given the mandate to be the *Missionary Man* who would visit all nations with the truth imparted to him by Shem his brother. Unique as it may appear this relay will be finished by all parties

involved so that Shem, Ham and Japheth finish the race together, i.e. all the civilization through Ham led to the fast communication of the Gospel which was given by God to Shem (via Abraham), preached to all the world through the Japhetic (European) missionaries.

There is one point which troubles my mind as I ponder upon this heavy subject. The religious face of Europe and America today is taking a sad twist in that most of the worship centers have either been abandoned or converted to beer halls or other use which has nothing to do with worshipping God at all. This is pathetic. In case you visit a church during worship you discover that there is a very small membership, whose composition is mainly old people of fifty years and beyond. What has happened to the children of Japheth, our former missionary? Has Christ's return been so much delayed that the missionaries have forgotten their mandate, or have they grown so weary of the gospel so much that they neglect God's call?

In those churches in America and Europe, those who still attend church are mostly from the children of Ham. Prophecy is fast fulfilling that in the last days Africa will stretch out her hands to God. The children of Japheth are still however called upon to worship God and continue spreading the Good News, proclaiming the mighty works of the Lord, declaring what He has done to all humanity.

It should be noted that each son of Noah in the same relay had his own unique share of misdeeds and evil hence they today all need the cleansing blood of the Lamb; The

Lamb that was slain before the foundation of the world (Rom 3:23,24). This means that the descendents of Shem, Ham, and Japheth all can only be justified by faith in Jesus Christ, the Lord of all.

"What shall we conclude then? Are we any better? Not at all! We have already made the charge that Jews and Gentiles alike are all under sin. As it is written:

'There is no one righteous, not even one; there is no one who understands, no one who seeks God. All have turned away, they have together become worthless; there is no one who does good, not even one'"(Romans 3:9-12).

"You are all sons of God through faith in Christ Jesus, for all of you who were baptized into Christ have clothed yourself with Christ. There is neither Jew nor Greek, slave nor free, male nor female, for you are all one in Christ Jesus. If you belong to Christ then you are Abraham's seed and heirs according to the promise" (Gal 3:26-29).

JUSTIFIED BY FAITH

"Consider Abraham; he believed God, and it was credited to him as righteousness. Understand then that those who believe are children of Abraham. The scripture foresaw that God would justify the Gentiles by faith, and announced the gospel in advance to Abraham: 'All nations will be blessed through you'. So those who have faith are blessed along with Abraham, the man of faith" (Galatians 3: 6-9).

'If you belong to Christ, then you are Abraham's seed and heirs according to the promise' (Galatians 3: 29). The book of Romans also has much to say with regards to the race issue: "It is not as though God's word had failed. For not all who are descendants from Israel are Israel. Nor because they are his descendents are they all Abraham's children. On the contrary, it is through Isaac that your offspring will be reckoned. In other words it is not the natural children who are God's children, but it is the children of the promise who are regarded as Abraham's offspring…. Even us whom he also called, not only from the Jews but also from the Gentiles, as He says in Hosea: I will call them 'my people' who are not my people; and I will call her 'my loved one' who is not my loved one, It will happen that in the very place where it was said to them, 'You are not my people' they will be called 'sons of the Living God'" (Romans 9: 6-8, 24-26).

CHRIST HAS DESTROYED THE EVIL BARRIER

"Therefore remember that formerly you who are Gentiles by birth and called 'uncircumcised' by those who call themselves 'the circumcision' (that done in the body by the hands of men)- remember that at that time you were separate from Christ, excluded from citizenship in Israel and foreigners to the covenants of the promise, without hope and without God in the world. But now in Christ Jesus you who once were far away have been brought near through the blood of Christ. For He Himself is our peace, who has made the two, one and has destroyed the barrier, the dividing wall of hostility, by abolishing in His flesh the law with its commandments and regulations. His purpose was to create in Himself one new man out of the two, thus making peace, and in this one body, to reconcile both of them to God through the cross, by which He put to death their hostility. He came and preached peace to you who were far away and peace to those who were near. For through Him we both have access to the father by one spirit (Ephesians 2:11-18).

THE COVENANT OF GRACE

The Covenant of Grace was first made with man in Eden, where after the fall, there was given a divine promise that the seed of the woman would crush the serpent's head (Gen 3:15). To all humanity this covenant offered pardon for future obedience through faith in Jesus Christ. There was also enshrined in the same covenant of grace, eternal life through faith in Jesus Christ and keeping His eternal Law, The Ten Commandments.

E. G White confirms that this is the same covenant which God renewed with Abraham in the promise, "and through your offspring all nations on earth will be blessed, because you have obeyed me" (Genesis 22;18). This promise definitely pointed to Christ. The Covenant of Grace which includes **all nations, tribes and kindred and tongue was ratified by the death of Jesus Christ on the cross of Calvary in A.D. 31**. This was then entitled the Second or The New Covenant coming after The First and Old Covenant. This is so because the blood that was shed on the cross of Calvary to ratify the Covenant was shed after the blood of the first covenant,(that of animal sacrifices) {Heb 6:17,18}. The grace of God is so amazing that even the vilest of sinners in any barbaric nation is bidden to come and enjoy the benefits and merits of the blood of Jesus. Fellow, African, there is definitely no excuse for denying this **free grace, which is so marvelous. It conquers all our guilt and shame. Grace that is greater than all our sins**.

'For the grace of God that brings salvation has appeared to all men. It teaches us to say 'No' to ungodliness, and worldly passions, and to live self-controlled, upright and godly lives in this present age, while we wait for this blessed hope—the glorious appearing of our great God and Savior, Jesus Christ, who gave Himself for us to redeem us from all wickedness, and to purify for Himself a people that are His very own, eager to do what is good (Titus 2:11-14).

CONCLUSION

Being aware of our Black Biblical heritage awakens us to see and understand that God used Africans extensively in the Bible so as to achieve His purpose. God does not segregate people on any grounds (Acts 10: 34-35). Surprisingly the Bible speaks more of the seed of Ham than that of Japheth.

> Talking on God's choices, we know that He called the children of Israel (Sons of Shem), exalted them not that by obedience to His law they alone might receive His favor and become the exclusive recipients of His blessings; but in order to reveal Himself through them to all the inhabitants of the earth. It was for the accomplishment of this very purpose that He commanded them to keep themselves distinct from the idolatrous nations around them. This is what Enoch, Noah, Abraham, Joseph, and Moses did, and it is just what God designed that His people Israel should do (*emphasis mine*) {Patriarchs and Prophets, 1890, p. 369}.

"Come now, let us reason together, says the Lord. Thou your sins are like scarlet, they shall be as white as snow; thou they are red as crimson, they shall be as wool. If you are willing and obedient you will eat the best from the land; but if you resist and rebel, you will be devoured by the sword" (Isaiah 1:18,19).

BIBLIOGRAPHY

Atmore, A. et el. *The Readers Digest History of Man.* London: The Readers Digest Association, 1973.

Ayandele, A. Afigbo, E., Gavin, R. J. and Professor J.D. Omer- Cooper. *The Growth of African Civilizations: The Making of Modern Africa.* Harare: Longman, 1985.

Bankole, Timothy. *Missionary Shepherds and African Sheep.* Badan: Daystar Press, 1971.

Evans, Anthony. T. *Are Blacks Spiritually Inferior To Whites?: The Dispelling of an African Myth.* U.S.A.: Renaissance Productions, Inc.,1992.

Jackson, H.C. *Ethiopia and the Origin of Civilization.* New York:N.P.,1974.

Jenkins, C. *The Black Hebrews.* U.S.A.: The Westminster Press, 1969.

Johnson, L. John. *The Black Biblical Heritage.* Nashville, Tennessee: Winston-Derek Publishers, Inc. 1945.

McCray, Walter Arthur. *The Black Presence in the Bible and the Table of Nations.* Chicago: Black Light Fellowship,1990.

Parker, B.M. *Fascinating Facts: A Treasury of Information on Hundreds of Subjects.* London: Hamlyn Publishing Group Limited, 1970.

The Message Magazine." *Culture and History of the Black Experience*". Nashville: Southern Publishing Association, 1974.

Rwodzi, G. *Kuzarura Zvakazarurwa.* Harare, Zimbabwe: Rothmar Enterprises (Pvt) Ltd. 2011.

White, E. G. *The Great Controversy.* Washington D.C.: Review and Herald Publishing Asssociation, 1956.

------------------.*Partriarchs and Prophets.* Washington D.C.: Review and Herald Publishing Association, 1948.